The Genius Of THE STONE, BRONZE, AND IRON AGES

INNOVATIONS FROM PAST CIVILIZATIONS

NEW HANOVER COUNTY PUBLIC LIBRARY

IZZI HOWELL

CRABTREE PUBLISHING COMPANY
WWW.CRABTREEBOOKS.COM

Published in Canada
Crabtree Publishing
616 Welland Avenue
St. Catharines, ON
L2M 5V6

Published in the United States
Crabtree Publishing
PMB 59051
350 Fifth Ave, 59th Floor
New York, NY 10118

Published in 2020 by Crabtree Publishing Company

All rights reserved. No part of this publication may be reproduced, stored in a retrieval system or be transmitted in any form or by any means, electronic, mechanical, photocopying, recording, or otherwise, without the prior written permission of the copyright owner.

First published in Great Britain in 2019 by The Watts Publishing Group
Copyright © The Watts Publishing Group 2019

Author: Izzi Howell

Editorial director: Kathy Middleton

Editors: Izzi Howell, Petrice Custance

Proofreader: Melissa Boyce

Series Designer: Rocket Design (East Anglia) Ltd

Designer: Clare Nicholas

Prepress technician: Tammy McGarr

Print coordinator: Katherine Berti

Consultant: Philip Parker

Printed in the U.S.A./072019/CG20190501

Photo credits:
Alamy: Heritage Image Partnership Ltd 7b, North Wind Picture Archives 9r, INTERFOTO 16, Ladi Kirn 23b; Getty: JUSTIN TALLIS/AFP 4t, HomoCosmicos 5b, Maltaguy1 10, English Heritage/Heritage Images 11t, 11b, 13 and 17, A-S-L 12br, Dean Mouhtaropoulos 19, De Agostini Picture Library/De Agostini 22, Henglein and Steets 28; Julian Baker 23t; Metropolitan Museum (public domain): Rogers Fund, 1999 3b and 25b, Dodge Fund, 1933 21t and 25t; Shutterstock: Brian C. Weed cover, Jule_Berlin title page and 18, pzAxe 3t, dikobraziy 4b, Diego Fiore 3t, Jason Benz Bennee 3c, arka38 6, mountainpix 7t, hapelena 8, Alena Brozova 9l, Alex Coan 12t, Alfonso de Tomas 12bl, Philip Bird LRPS CPAGB 14, Mr Nai 15 and 30, UAV 4 17, Bjoern Wylezich 20l, ntv 20r, Nataliya Nazarova 21b, EQRoy 24, Kamira 26, Fedor Selivanov 29; Walters Art Museum: Museum purchase, 1941 28c.

All design elements from Shutterstock.

Every attempt has been made to clear copyright. Should there be any inadvertent omission please apply to the publisher for rectification.

The website addresses (URLs) included in this book were valid at the time of going to press. However, it is possible that contents or addresses may have changed since the publication of this book. No responsibility for any such changes can be accepted by either the author or the Publisher.

Library and Archives Canada Cataloguing in Publication

Title: The genius of the Stone, Bronze, and Iron Ages / Izzi Howell.
Names: Howell, Izzi, author.
Series: Genius of the ancients.
Description: Series statement: The genius of the ancients | Includes index.
Identifiers: Canadiana (print) 20190108533 |
  Canadiana (ebook) 20190108568 |
  ISBN 9780778765776 (hardcover) |
  ISBN 9780778765974 (softcover) |
  ISBN 9781427123947 (HTML)
Subjects: LCSH: Civilization, Ancient—Juvenile literature. | LCSH: Stone age—Juvenile literature. | LCSH: Bronze age—Juvenile literature. | LCSH: Iron age—Juvenile literature. | LCSH: Technological innovations—Juvenile literature.
Classification: LCC CB311 .H69 2019 | DDC j930—dc23

Library of Congress Cataloging-in-Publication Data

Names: Howell, Izzi, author.
Title: The genius of the Stone, Bronze, and Iron Ages / Izzi Howell.
Description: New York, New York : Crabtree Publishing Company, 2020. | Series: The genius of the ancients | Audience: Ages: 9-12. | Audience: Grades: 4-6. | Includes index. |
Identifiers: LCCN 2019014241 (print) | LCCN 2019018665 (ebook) | ISBN 9781427123947 (Electronic) | ISBN 9780778765776 (hardcover) | ISBN 9780778765974 (pbk.)
Subjects: LCSH: Civilization, Ancient--Juvenile literature. | Stone age--Juvenile literature. | Bronze age--Juvenile literature. | Iron age--Juvenile literature. | Technological innovations--Juvenile literature.
Classification: LCC CB311 (ebook) | LCC CB311 .H67 2020 (print) | DDC 930--dc23
LC record available at https://lccn.loc.gov/2019014241

CONTENTS

THE STONE, BRONZE, AND IRON AGES → 4
STONE → 6
BRONZE → 8
IRON → 10
FARMING → 12
CONSTRUCTION → 14
SETTLEMENTS → 16
SOCIETY → 18
TRADE → 20
CLOTHING → 22
ART → 24
THE WHEEL → 26
WRITING → 28
GLOSSARY → 30
TIMELINE → 31
INDEX AND LEARNING MORE → 32

THE STONE, BRONZE, AND IRON AGES

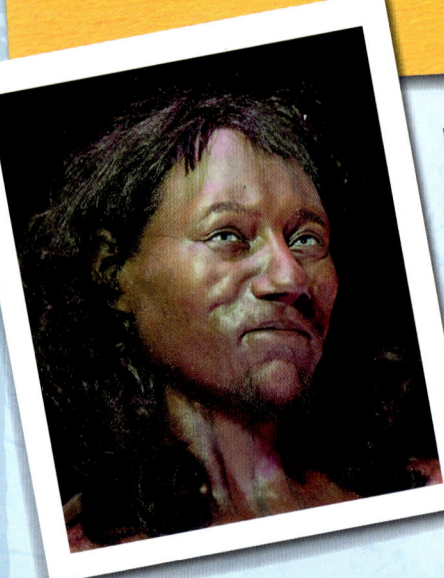

Who?

The Stone, Bronze, and Iron Ages cover a long period of history. They stretch from the time of the first **ancestors** of modern humans, who lived over two million years ago, through to the first modern humans and up to the time of the ancient **civilizations**. It was a period of great discovery and change, as humans began to use tools, grow crops, and work with metal. These **inventions** had a huge impact on **prehistoric** life.

This is a **reconstruction** of the face of a man who lived in Britain 10,000 years ago.

This map shows how and when early humans traveled and settled across the globe.

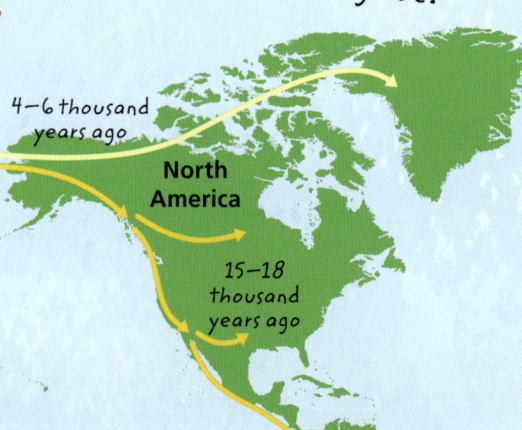

Europe 40–45 thousand years ago

Asia

4–6 thousand years ago

North America

15–18 thousand years ago

Africa 60–65 thousand years ago

Australia 50–55 thousand years ago

South America 15 thousand years ago

What happened?

The names "Stone Age," "Bronze Age," and "Iron Age" are terms that historians use to divide up different stages in history. The Stone Age is defined by the use of stone tools, while people worked with bronze during the Bronze Age, and then began using iron tools in the Iron Age.

This Bronze Age **pottery** model of a horse-drawn **chariot** was found in what is now Lebanon.

Bronze and Iron Age people also worked with other metals, such as gold.

Where?

The Stone, Bronze, and Iron Ages began and finished at different times around the world. For example, the Iron Age began 500 years earlier in the Middle East than in Europe. In Europe, the end of the Iron Age is considered the start of the great ancient civilizations, such as the ancient Greeks and Romans. Some areas never went through certain periods. People in South America did not work with bronze or iron, and therefore did not experience the Bronze or Iron Ages.

The Great Ziggurat of Ur was built by the Sumerian civilization in Mesopotamia (modern-day Iraq) in the Bronze Age. The building has been restored to show what it would have looked like thousands of years ago.

STONE

The ancestors of modern humans began to use stones as tools around 2.5 million years ago in Africa. This marked the beginning of the Stone Age. During the Stone Age, humans learned how to turn stones into useful and increasingly effective tools.

Chipping away

The very first stone tools were stones that had been naturally chipped. Humans used the sharp chipped edge as a blade for cutting. It took time to find rocks that were naturally chipped, so people began to chip the rocks themselves to create cutting tools. They used another stone to chip away flakes of rock from one side of a round stone. This created a rough **serrated** edge that could be used to cut meat or dig roots up out of the ground.

Early stone tools had rough, irregular blades.

(((Brain Wave)))

The first stone toolmakers used a hard stone to shape tools. Later, they figured out that some rocks could be chipped using softer materials. One technique was to use a long piece of bone or horn to gently chip away very small pieces of rock. This created a much smoother blade.

Axes and beyond

Over time, humans realized that chipping away both sides of a stone made a sharper and more effective blade. These tools were known as hand axes. Humans took the idea of the hand ax and developed it into different types of blades, such as knives, arrowheads, and tools for scraping. These blades could cut through wood, bone, and horn.

Sophisticated stones

Adding handles to stone tools made them much easier to hold. It also meant they could be swung, which enabled people to apply more pressure when cutting. This helped them to cut up thick tree trunks. Stone Age people also learned how to make smoother tools by polishing them on a rough rock. A smooth blade was sharper, which meant that it could cut deeper and more accurately.

This Stone Age hand ax has two sharpened sides. It is made from flint, a type of rock that was often used for tools in the Stone Age.

To keep up with the demand for flint tools, Stone Age people **mined** flint from the ground. This drawing shows Grime's Graves, a flint mine in Britain. There, miners dug deep holes and picked flint out of the ground using horn tools.

BRONZE

Around 4000 B.C.E., in what is now the Middle East, the prehistoric world took a huge step forward when people started to produce bronze. By about 2000 B.C.E., bronze tools and the knowledge of how to make them had spread to Europe.

GENIUS METAL MELTING

pure copper

Copper

Before people started using bronze, they worked with copper. Getting hold of pure copper was fairly simple, as solid pieces of pure copper can sometimes be found in nature. However, copper was too soft for weapons and tools. So, people experimented with copper and learned that they could produce a much stronger metal by combining it with other substances. The resulting metal was bronze.

Melting and molds

To make bronze, metalworkers had to **extract** pure metal from copper and tin ores, which are rocks that contain metals and other substances. First, they crushed the ore into small pieces. Then, they heated the ore over a charcoal fire to melt the metal. The melted metal could then be separated from the rock and mixed with other substances to make bronze. The melted bronze was poured into **molds**, where it hardened into solid bronze.

(((BRAIN WAVE)))

Bronze is an alloy, which means it is a mixture of different **elements**, including at least one metal. Bronze is mainly made up of copper, to which other elements are added. The first bronze was made by combining copper with a poisonous substance called arsenic. Later, people learned that combining copper with tin made a stronger bronze alloy.

Melted bronze can be poured into molds to produce a variety of objects, such as knives and ax-heads.

TEST OF TIME

The use of molds made it possible for Bronze Age people to make many copies of exactly the same bronze item. Factories today also use molds to create products. Using the same mold means you can easily and quickly create the same product over and over again.

The rise of bronze

At first, bronze was extremely valuable because it was rare. Few people knew how to create bronze objects, so they were hard to come by. Also, it could only be produced in areas rich in metal. Only wealthy people could afford bronze objects, such as jewelry. As bronze became more widely available because of metal-trading routes (see page 21), new weapons, such as the sword, were developed. For the first time in history, warriors wore protective metal armor, including helmets and shields.

Rich Europeans from the Bronze Age showed off their wealth by wearing bronze jewelry, belt buckles, and cloak brooches. They also carried bronze swords and daggers.

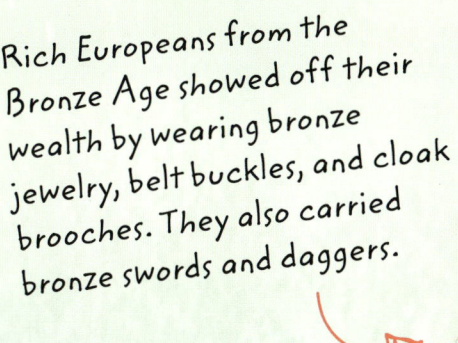

IRON

People began to make iron around 1200 B.C.E. in the Middle East and southwestern Europe. By 700 B.C.E., ironworking had spread across Europe. Iron was more easily available than bronze, which made strong iron tools and weapons more accessible to many Iron Age people.

A different process

Iron ore is more common than copper and tin ores, so Iron Age people didn't have to **import** the ore from other areas. However, extracting iron from its ore is more difficult than copper or tin. Iron Age people found that iron could not be melted and poured like bronze. Instead, pieces of iron ore had to be heated to a very high temperature with charcoal. Then, the pieces were hammered into shape while red-hot.

WOW!

The first iron used to make tools was taken from meteorites that fell to Earth from space! These **meteorites** were pure iron, so the metal didn't have to be separated from ore before it could be used. Meteorite iron was used in the Middle East and China.

*This modern **blacksmith** is hammering iron while it is red-hot to create its shape. This is the same technique that was used in the Iron Age.*

Iron Age people used iron to make weapons, cooking pots, and utensils.

From bronze to iron

Bronze weapons and tools were replaced with iron ones fairly quickly. This may have been due to improved methods of travel and contact with other people, which helped iron-making **technology** spread quickly. It may have also been due to a shortage of tin, which prevented people from making bronze. The strength and availability of iron made it the obvious choice for new weapons and tools.

Farming with iron

Iron tools and weapons were stronger and more effective than those made of bronze. Iron Age people used their new iron tools to cut down large numbers of trees to create more farmland. They then used iron farming tools to break up the heavy soil so they could grow crops. In this way, the development of iron tools helped them to produce more food and support a larger number of people.

Iron Age farmers used iron-tipped wooden plows to prepare the fields before planting seeds.

FARMING

In around 10,000 B.C.E., Stone Age people began to farm the land and grow crops, rather than just eating wild foods. This change had a huge impact on **society**, affecting the movement of people, population size, and settlements.

GENIUS ★ STABLE FOOD SUPPLY

Hunter-gatherers

The first humans were hunter-gatherers. They moved around looking for wild food, including animals to hunt, and leaves, fruits, and roots to collect. The food they ate depended on their location and the season—for example, berries in autumn. If food was hard to find, a group would move on to a new location.

Blackberries, birds' eggs, and young nettles are some wild foods that Stone Age people would have eaten.

The first farmers

Around 10,000 B.C.E., people in Turkey, the Middle East, and Mesopotamia began to farm. They planted fields of crops, such as barley and early types of wheat. They **domesticated** animals, such as sheep, goats, and cattle, for their meat and milk. These farms allowed people to produce much more food than they could have collected in the wild. Over time, farming spread across Asia and Europe.

A changing world

The development of farming led to changes in society. Humans could grow enough food to support a larger population. As a result, the number of humans grew around the world. Groups had to settle in one place to look after their farms. They built permanent villages next to their fields with more **complex** houses and structures (see page 14).

Brain Wave

The first farmers grew crops from wild seeds. They watered the plants and helped them to grow. Later, they collected new seeds from the fruit produced by the plant. Over time, they learned how to select the best seeds. They only planted seeds that had been collected from the strongest plants that produced large amounts of crops.

This artist's impression shows a Bronze Age farming village in around 2000 B.C.E.

CONSTRUCTION

When humans settled down in one place to farm in the late Stone Age and Bronze Age, they built permanent structures to live in. Farming freed up extra time for people to experiment with different building materials and other types of structures.

Simple shelters

As hunter-gatherers did not stay in one place for long, they built quick, temporary shelters. They set up camp in the mouths of caves or built simple structures from leaves, sticks, and animal skins. Later in the Stone Age, some groups would return to the same place every year. They started to build larger camps that they could come back to.

Construction techniques

When farmers started to build permanent settlements, they put more time and energy into constructing better shelters, as they knew they would be there for some time. These shelters looked different around the world, depending on the materials available, such as wood, stone, or mud. People developed different building techniques using these materials. Some made bricks from dried mud, or packed dried straw closely together to make a **thatched** roof.

In the Bronze Age, people in Europe built permanent houses from wood and thatch.

TEST OF TIME

Mud bricks are still used for construction in some parts of the world. They are made by mixing mud, sand, and water with straw, and leaving it to dry in wooden molds. The mixture hardens into a strong brick. Mud bricks are cheap and **durable**, and they keep the inside of a building cool during the day and warm at night.

Monuments and megaliths

As well as houses, people began to construct other types of buildings. Many groups of people around the world built huge monuments, often for religious reasons. These monuments were typically made of giant stones called megaliths. In the Bronze Age, the Sumerians built huge buildings called ziggurats in Mesopotamia. The bricks in the ziggurats were arranged in steps that got gradually smaller toward the top.

(((BRAIN WAVE)))

Historians aren't sure how the makers of Stonehenge lifted the very heavy stones. They may have built wooden **scaffolding** to lift them up bit by bit or pushed them up on ramps. However they did it, it was a brilliant piece of **engineering** work!

Stonehenge in England has a ring of standing megaliths, some with stones balanced on top.

SETTLEMENTS

Over time, the first Stone Age farming settlements grew into small villages. These villages became centers for work, with workshops for craftspeople. In the Bronze and Iron Ages, some of these villages grew into towns and even cities, where thousands of people lived close together.

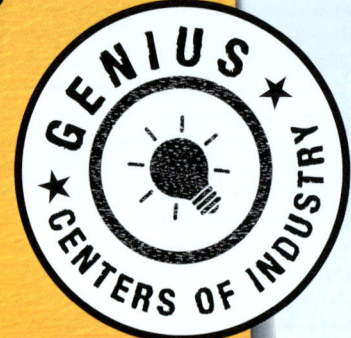

GENIUS ★ CENTERS OF INDUSTRY

WOW! The site of the current city of Jericho, Palestine, has been lived in for 10,000 years. This makes it one of the oldest continuously inhabited towns in the world!

New roles

With the development of farming, fewer people were needed to produce enough food to feed a large population. This freed up people to work on other projects. Some became **potters**, craftspeople, and metalworkers, producing pots, fabric, and weapons. Others became warriors to defend their village against attacks from other tribes.

People in a Stone Age farming village had different roles. Some were farmers, while others made tools, caught fish, or prepared food.

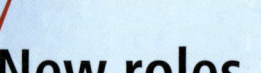

This hill fort was built in the southwest of England during the Iron Age. Families lived in houses at the top of the central mound.

Keeping safe

Towns and cities offered protection to Bronze and Iron Age people. There was safety in numbers, as warriors and men from the town would defend it in the event of an attack. Defensive walls were built around some settlements to keep residents safe.

(((Brain Wave)))

High settlements are easier to defend, as you can see your enemies coming and have the advantage of fighting battles downhill. In Bronze and Iron Age Europe, some groups built forts on tall hills. They dug ditches around their settlements to make it even harder for attackers to reach them at the top.

Special towns

Over time, some Bronze and Iron Age towns and cities began to **specialize**. Settlements near **natural resources**, such as metal, became manufacturing centers. People who lived there trained to work with that area's resources. Settlements near rivers or along the coast became trading centers (see page 21). Traders brought in new goods from far away, and **exchanged** them for locally produced objects.

SOCIETY

During the Stone, Bronze, and Iron Ages, society changed from being basically equal to **hierarchical**, with rulers at the top and others in order of importance beneath them. Leaders enjoyed a comfortable lifestyle, but ordinary people did not share the same luxuries as those at the top.

An equal society?

Historians can only guess about the society of the early Stone Age humans. As hunter-gatherers, everyone in society had the same responsibility—collect and prepare food to eat. For this reason, most people probably saw each other as equals. **Archaeologists** have found evidence that even in the late Stone Age, people lived in houses of the same size. This is a sign of a basically equal society.

Skara Brae is a Stone Age village on the Scottish island of Orkney. The houses that remain are all exactly the same size and have the same features.

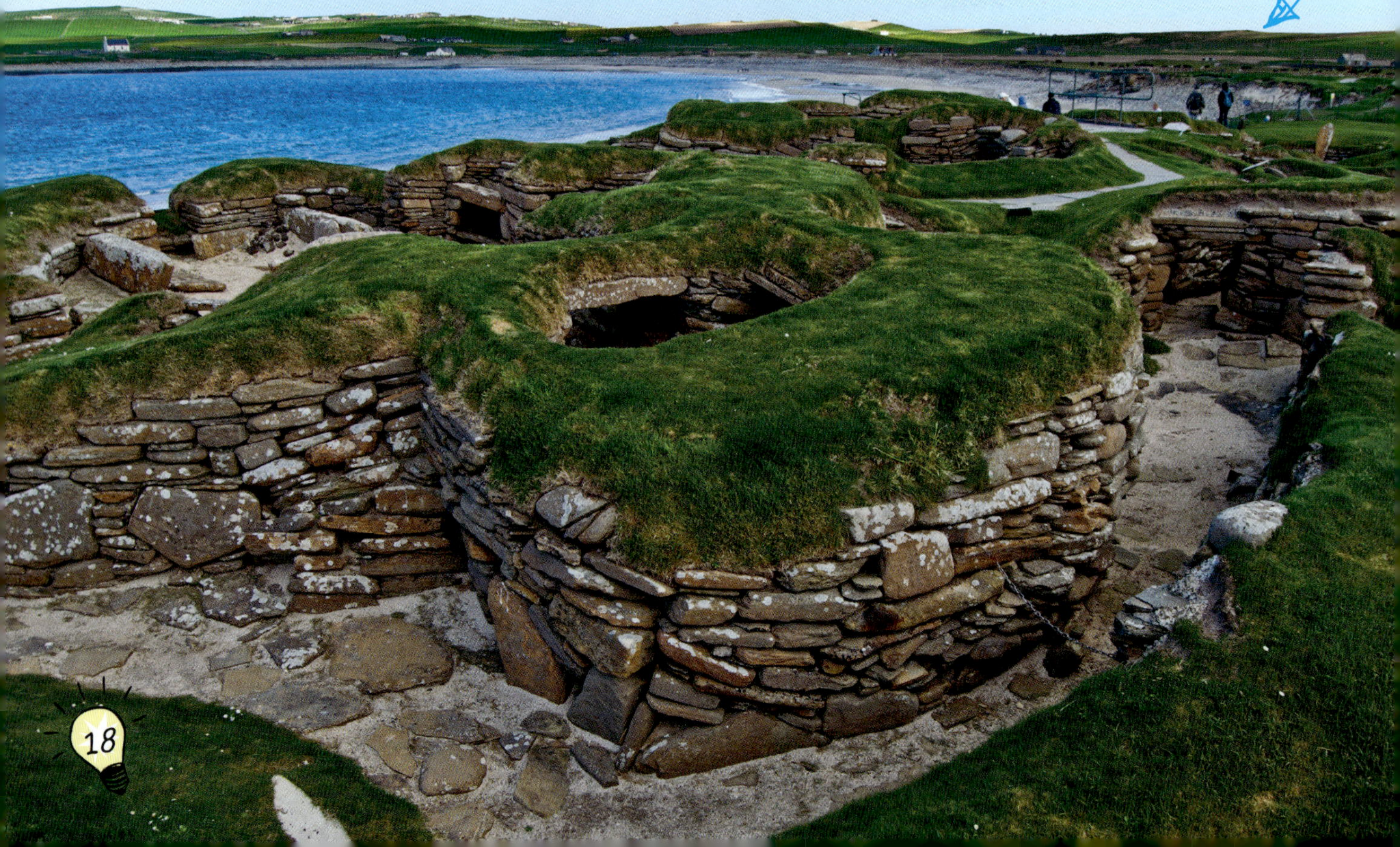

The beginnings of wealth

As farming became widespread, the people who controlled the extra food produced became powerful and wealthy. When bronze was introduced, these powerful people were the first to obtain metal objects. This was the beginning of a hierarchical society. The people at the top of society had valuable items and more food, while ordinary people lived much simpler and more basic lives.

WOW! Archaeologists have used evidence found in graves to identify powerful Bronze and Iron Age people. Important members of society were buried with valuable metal objects. From their skeletons, we can also tell whether the person had a good diet, another sign of wealth and comfort.

This is a recreation of a Bronze Age grave found in Varna, Bulgaria. The person was buried with many gold items, probably because of their high status.

Iron Age hierarchy

By the beginning of the Iron Age, there were many different roles in society, each with its own level of importance. Tribal leaders were at the top, followed by **noble** people and priests. Below them were warriors and skilled craftspeople. Landless laborers and enslaved people were at the bottom. People from each part of society lived in houses of different sizes, wore different clothes, and ate different foods.

- tribal leaders/kings
- noble people
- priests
- warriors
- skilled craftspeople
- farmers/fishers
- landless laborers and enslaved people

TRADE

In the late Stone Age and early Bronze Age, people began to trade with each other to share resources. Groups traded extra food supplies, craft products, and specific resources, such as tin, that could only be found in certain areas.

GENIUS RESOURCE SHARING

Stone Age sharing

After the introduction of farming, Stone Age people had extra food for the first time. Some food was dried and stored for later use, while some was traded with other groups in the local area. People also traded items, such as craft products. Many craft products could be made for trading due to the extra time freed up by farming.

WOW!
Archaeologists have found Stone Age jade axes in Scotland that originally came from the Italian Alps!

Valuable stones, such as obsidian from the Greek islands, and amber from Poland, were traded across Stone Age Europe.

obsidian

amber

Trading tin

In the Bronze Age, trading became very important because tin, one of the **raw materials** needed for bronze, was only found in a few areas. Most Bronze Age people depended on trade to be able to access the tin needed to make bronze tools and weapons. Bronze Age traders across Europe and Asia became rich from trading tin, as well as **precious metals** and **textiles**.

This necklace, found in a Sumerian royal tomb, is made from traded, non-local materials. It has beads made from blue stones called lapis lazuli, from what is now Afghanistan, and gold from what is now Iran and Turkey.

Land and sea

By the Iron Age, a network of trade routes had been established across Europe, allowing goods to be transported by land or sea. This gave people access to a wider variety of foods and objects. Commonly traded goods included salt and amber, a gemstone used for jewelry. Iron Age tribes traded goods with each other, as well as with large civilizations, such as the ancient Greeks.

*Iron Age traders in the Mediterranean probably used simple wooden ships, similar to this modern **replica**.*

CLOTHING

We don't have much information about the clothing worn during the Stone, Bronze, and Iron Ages. Most ancient textiles have rotted away and are very rarely found. However, by looking at the technologies used to make clothes, we can guess what people wore.

Knives and needles

The first humans kept warm by covering themselves in animal skins. They used stone knives to cut the skin from the animals. The development of needles, made from bone or horn, enabled people to make holes in these skins. They could now make fitted clothes from animal skins sewn together with thin pieces of leather or plants. These clothes kept people warmer, which allowed them to travel into colder **climates**.

This artwork shows Stone Age people in different clothes made from animal skins, including boots to protect their feet.

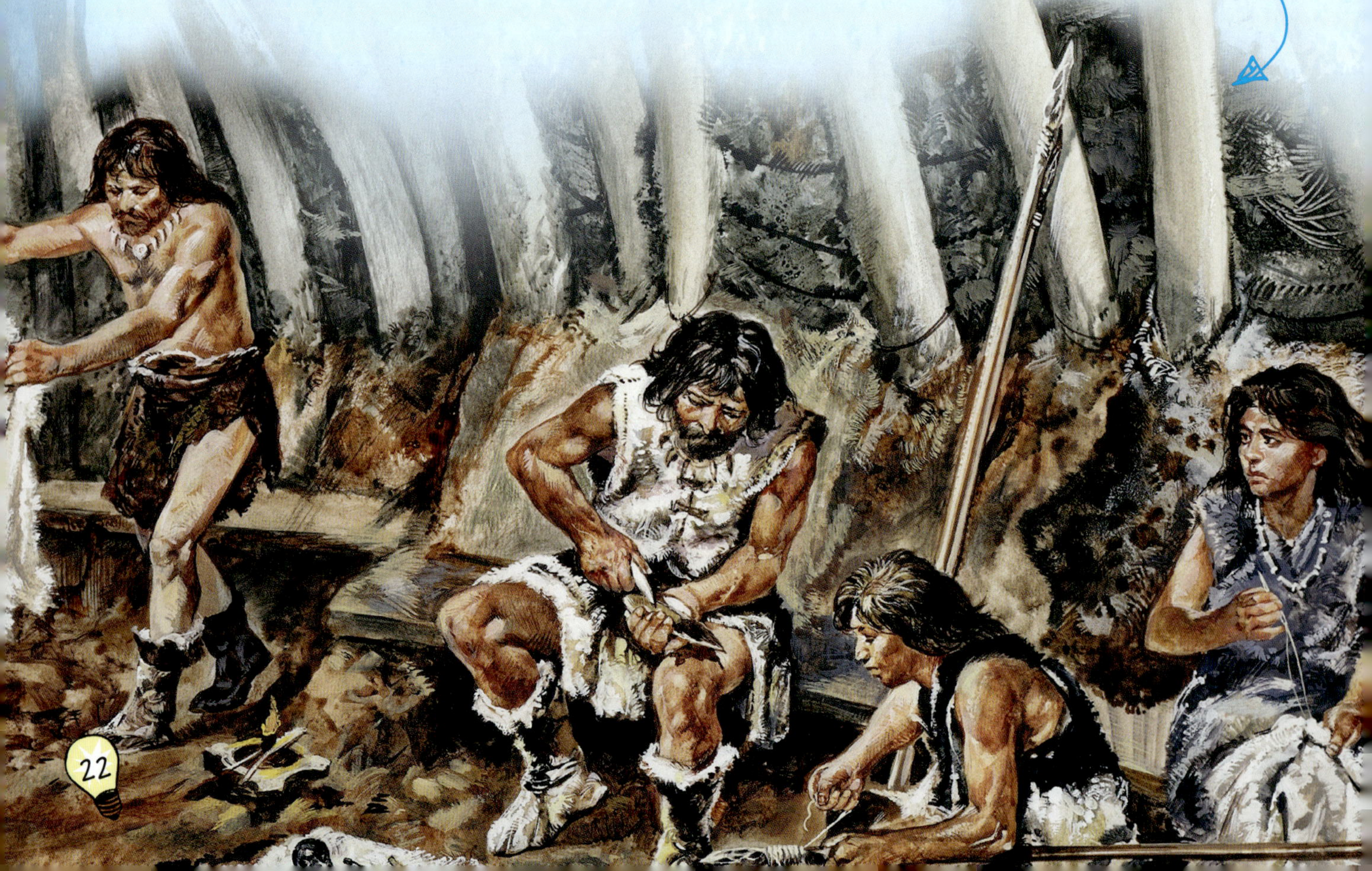

Weaving

Over time, people started making their own material. They made baskets and fishing nets from plant fibers. By 5000 B.C.E., people were **weaving** cloth fabric from threads made from plant and animal fibers. The threads used to make cloth varied around the world. In India, they used cotton, while in China, they used silk. People in other areas, such as Britain, wove cloth from wool. They used natural dyes from plants to color the cloth.

BRAIN WAVE

At first, people made thread by hand. They rolled animal hair or plants in their hands until it became thin threads. Making thread became easier later in the Stone Age, due to the invention of the drop spindle (see right). A drop spindle is a weighted stick, through which fibers are threaded.

The weight of the spindle pulls the fiber into thin thread when it is spun. The thread is then wrapped around the spindle.

The loom

Stone Age people used looms to weave fabric. A loom was a wooden frame that was set up with strings of thread hanging **vertically** from the top. Stones were tied to the bottom of each string to keep it straight. Threads were woven **horizontally** back and forth between the vertical threads to create large pieces of woven fabric. These large pieces of fabric could be made into different types of clothes.

This is a replica of an ancient loom. A weaver could walk around the loom while weaving to reach either side.

TEST OF TIME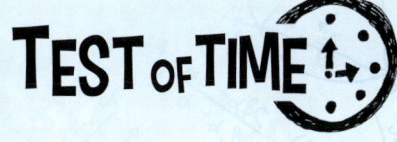

Woven fabric is still created in exactly the same way, with horizontal threads wrapped around vertical threads. However, since the **Industrial Revolution**, people have used mechanical looms that create fabric automatically. Some craftspeople still weave by hand, producing high-quality luxury fabrics.

ART

During the Stone Age, our human ancestors began making art. At first, the art was very simple. Then, throughout the Bronze Age and Iron Age, artists became more and more skilled. People began creating **intricately** decorated objects as symbols of wealth and power.

GENIUS CREATIVE TOUCHES

The first paintings

Cave painting was one of the earliest forms of art in the Stone Age. People painted pictures of animals, and occasionally humans, on walls deep inside caves. They used red, brown, and black paints, made from charcoal and soil. These paintings may have had a religious meaning.

This cave painting of a bison, located in Spain, was painted more than 15,000 years ago.

New materials

Every new material that humans learned how to work with was used to create art and decorative objects. In the Stone Age, people carved bone into figurines and beads for jewelry. After the development of pottery, people made decorative sculptures, as well as **functional** pots. In the Bronze and Iron Ages, craftspeople made brooches and rings from metal.

This Sumerian headdress is made from gold and stones. It dates back to around 2600 B.C.E.

Decorating the world

In the Bronze and Iron Ages, artistic decoration was also added to functional objects, such as weapons, chariots, and bowls. This decoration would have taken extra time and resources, making the decorated object more expensive. These objects would have been symbols of power, and only owned by wealthy people.

TEST OF TIME

Men and women around the world still wear jewelry made from the same materials that people used thousands of years ago, such as metal and colorful stones. Today, people also make jewelry from human-made materials, such as plastic.

This sword from roughly 60 B.C.E. is decorated with a warrior on the handle.

THE WHEEL

The invention of the wheel actually happened quite late. Humans were building complex boats and doing intricate metalwork before the wheel was invented.

This decorated Sumerian box, known as the Standard of Ur, shows soldiers and wheeled wagons on their way to battle. It dates back to 2600 B.C.E.

The first wheels

Some historians believe that the first wheels were potter's wheels built around 3500 B.C.E. in Mesopotamia. The potter smoothed each pot as it spun on the wheel, to make it a more regular shape. These wheels were solid disks with a hole in the center for the **axle**. The axle and the hole in the wheel had to be perfectly smooth or the wheel would not spin correctly.

Moving around

The first wheeled vehicles appeared in Mesopotamia around 3200 B.C.E. They were possibly inspired by potter's wheels, or by log rollers used to move heavy objects. Wheeled vehicles made it much easier to transport heavy goods over long distances. Carts were pulled by oxen or donkeys, as there were no domesticated horses in Mesopotamia at the time. The wheels on these carts were solid wood, which made the vehicle quite heavy.

Riding into battle

Two developments—the invention of the spoked wheel and the domestication of the horse—were key to the invention of the horse-drawn chariot around 2000 B.C.E. Spoked wheels had rods connecting the center of the wheel to the rim, making them much lighter than solid wheels. Spoked wheels made the chariots easier to pull at faster speeds. Horses could also travel quicker than oxen, pulling the chariot at top speed. This made the chariot a valuable weapon in battle.

TEST OF TIME

Eventually, it became more common for soldiers to ride on horses in battle rather than use chariots. However, chariots were still used for transport and for entertainment, such as the popular chariot races in ancient Greece and Rome.

In battle, chariots were used to break through enemy lines. Soldiers then jumped off the chariots and fought hand to hand.

WRITING

The earliest humans communicated through spoken language. Humans communicated in this way for thousands of years before writing began. Writing was a huge step forward in human communication. People began to keep written records, from which we have learned a great deal about the lives of ancient people.

GENIUS COMMUNICATION RECORDS

Sumerian symbols

In ancient Mesopotamia in around 3400 B.C.E., people used small clay models to keep track of trade and farming records. These models were kept in clay envelopes. Eventually, people began to draw the contents of the envelope on the outside, which meant that the models weren't needed anymore. The drawing was enough to represent the information that the writer wanted to communicate. These symbols, or pictographs, were the first form of writing.

Sounding it out

However, there were some words and ideas that could not be drawn in a picture, such as names. So, the Sumerians started to use symbols for words that sounded the same to sound out words that couldn't be drawn. For example, the Sumerian word for hand was "su," so they drew a hand when they wanted to refer to a hand or to represent "su" when the sound appeared in other words.

The first writing was used for farming records, such as the amount of wheat **harvested** from a field.

vase

plants

This Sumerian tablet records the transfer of land. It's thought that the vase and foot symbols were used to represent sounds, while the image of plants represented a garden.

foot

Developing an alphabet

One of the first complete writing systems was ancient Egyptian **hieroglyphics**, which combined pictographs to represent objects and characters to represent sounds. This allowed people to keep detailed, accurate records of things that could not be drawn. Eventually, around 1500 B.C.E., **scribes** developed an alphabet in which each letter represented a sound. This system was more convenient as fewer symbols were needed.

TEST of TIME

As the ancient Romans conquered new lands, they introduced their Latin language and alphabet to the new territories. Today, the Latin alphabet is still the most-used writing system in the world.

Some Egyptian hieroglyphics represented objects and sounds. For example, the wavy line represented water and the "n" sound.

GLOSSARY

ancestor A relative who lived a long time ago

archaeologist A person who studies ancient cultures by examining sites and artifacts

axle The pole in the center of a circular object that allows it to spin around

blacksmith Someone who makes objects from iron or steel

chariot A horse-drawn vehicle used in ancient warfare and racing

civilization The stage of a human society, such as its culture and way of life

climate The weather conditions in a particular area

complex Involving many different but related parts

domesticate To control previously wild animals and use them for work

durable Able to last a long time without deteriorating

element A natural substance that cannot be broken down

engineering The design and building of machines and structures

exchange To trade one currency or valuable for another

extract To remove or pull a material out from something

functional Describes something that works or is able to be used

harvest To gather a crop

hierarchical Describes a system in which things are organized according to their importance

hieroglyphics The ancient Egyptian system of picture writing

horizontal A line running across, from side to side

import To receive goods for sale from a foreign area

Industrial Revolution A period beginning in the 1700s when many people began working with machines in factories

intricately Describes something done in a very complicated or highly detailed way

invention The creation of a new process or device

meteorite A rock that has fallen to Earth from space

mined Removed something from the earth

mold A frame that gives shape to something

natural resources Materials or substances from nature that can be used to earn money

noble To have a high rank or title

potter Someone who makes pottery

pottery Items made from baked clay

precious metal Highly valuable metals, such as gold and silver

prehistoric Describes the time before written records

raw material A natural material that has not yet been made into something else

reconstruction Something made to resemble the original as closely as possible

replica A copy of an original

scaffolding A set of ladders and platforms allowing people to work up high

scribe A person who writes documents by hand

serrated Describes a blade with several sharp points along its edge

society A group of people living together in a community

specialize To focus all efforts on one thing

technology Machinery and equipment developed from the use of scientific knowledge

textile A type of cloth or woven fabric

thatch A building material made of straw or dried plants

vertical A line running straight up and down

weaving The process of creating fabric by crossing threads together

TIMELINE

STONE AGE

2.5 million years ago	Stones are first used as tools.
10,000 B.C.E.	Farming begins in the Middle East.
9000 B.C.E.	The end of the last Ice Age brings warmer temperatures.

BRONZE AGE

4000 B.C.E.	The first bronze tools begin to be produced.
3500 B.C.E.	The first potter's wheels are used in Mesopotamia.
3400 B.C.E.	The earliest types of writing appear in ancient Mesopotamia and ancient Egypt.
2000 B.C.E.	The use of bronze becomes widespread across the Middle East and Europe.

IRON AGE

1200 B.C.E.	People begin to work with iron in the Middle East and southwestern Europe.
700 B.C.E.	Ironworking has spread across Europe.

INDEX

bronze 5, 8–9, 10, 11, 19, 21

chariots 5, 25, 27
clothing 19, 22–23
copper 8, 10
crafts 16, 17, 19, 20, 23, 25

farming 11, 12–13, 14, 16, 19, 20, 28

gold 5, 19, 21, 25

hill forts 17
hunter-gatherers 12, 14, 18

iron 5, 10–11

jewelry 9, 21, 25

paintings 24

shelters 14
ships 21
society 13, 18–19, 25
stone 5, 6–7, 14, 15, 20, 22, 23
Stonehenge 15
swords 9, 25

tin 8, 10, 11, 21
trade 17, 20–21, 28

villages 13, 16–17, 18

weaving 23
wheels 26–27
writing 28–29

ziggurats 5, 15

LEARNING MORE

Websites

www.dkfindout.com/us/history/stone-age/

https://kids.kiddle.co/Bronze_Age

www.dkfindout.com/us/history/iron-age/

Books

Doeden, Matt. *Tools and Treasures of Ancient Mesopotamia*. Lerner Classroom, 2014.

Rodger, Ellen. *Ancient Mesopotamia Inside Out*. Crabtree Publishing, 2017.

Taylor, Saranne. *Ancient Homes.* Crabtree Publishing, 2015.

NE   NOV   2019